S0-BHW-463

AMAZING MACHINES

CONCRETE MIXERS

BY QUINN M. ARNOLD

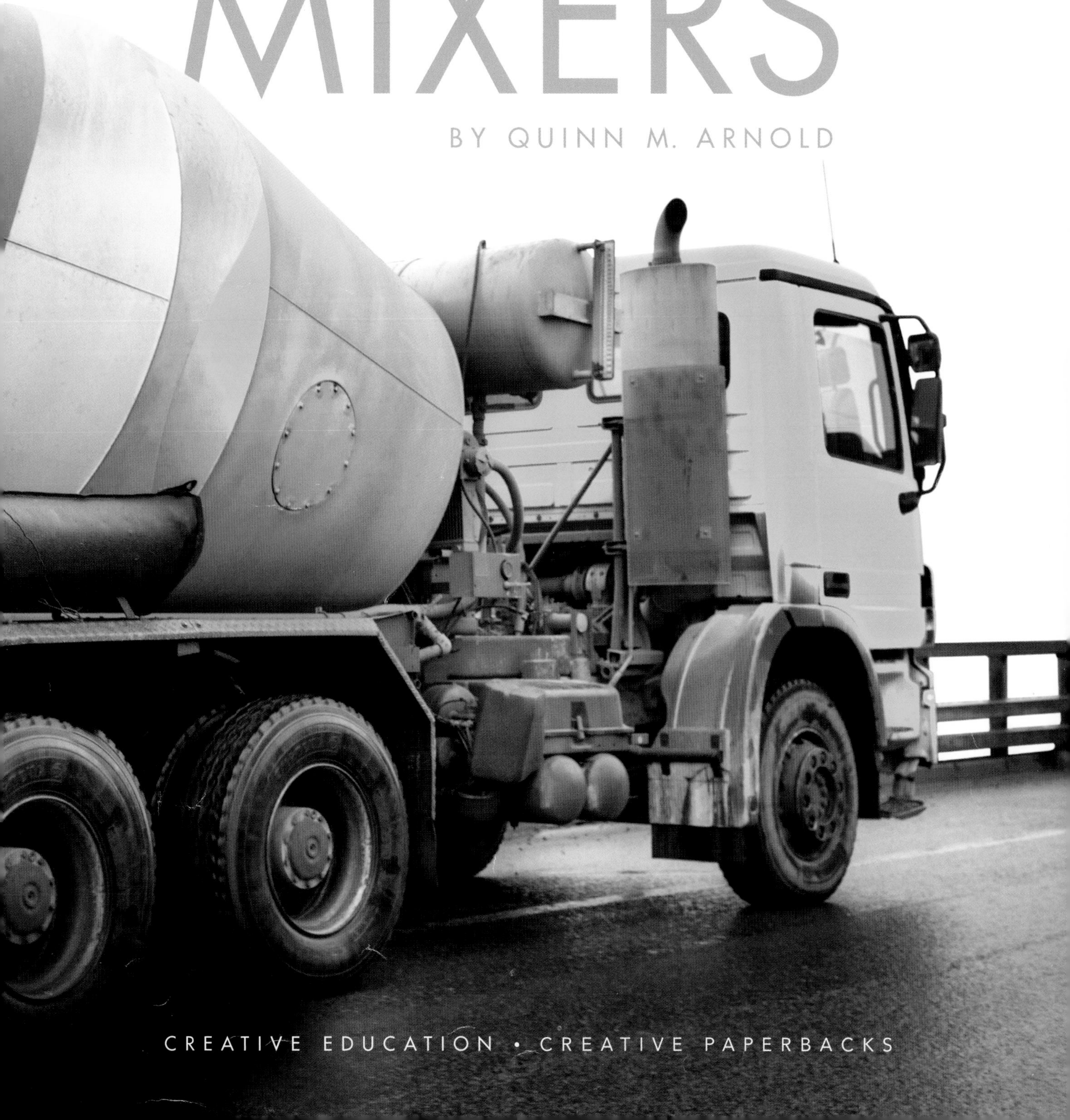

CREATIVE EDUCATION • CREATIVE PAPERBACKS

Published by Creative Education and Creative Paperbacks
P.O. Box 227, Mankato, Minnesota 56002
Creative Education and Creative Paperbacks are imprints of
The Creative Company
www.thecreativecompany.us

Design by The Design Lab
Production by Chelsey Luther
Art direction by Rita Marshall
Printed in the United States of America

Photographs by Alamy (Justin Kase zninez), Dreamstime (Stephen Coburn, Roman Milert), Getty Images (Hulton-Deutsch Collection/CORBIS, Westend61), iStockphoto (BanksPhotos, Elen11, ewg3D, kozmoat98, mbbirdy, rtyree1), Shutterstock (Bambuh, Eng. Bilal Izaddin, Orange Line Media)

Copyright © 2018 Creative Education, Creative Paperbacks
International copyright reserved in all countries. No part of this book may be reproduced in any form without written permission from the publisher.

Library of Congress Cataloging-in-Publication Data
Names: Arnold, Quinn M., author.
Title: Concrete mixers / Quinn M. Arnold.
Series: Amazing machines.
Includes bibliographical references and index.
Summary: A basic exploration of the parts, variations, and worksites of concrete mixers, the cement-mixing machines. Also included is a pictorial diagram of variations of concrete mixers.
Identifiers: ISBN 978-1-60818-887-1 (hardcover) / ISBN 978-1-62832-503-4 (pbk) / ISBN 978-1-56660-939-5 (eBook)
This title has been submitted for CIP processing under LCCN 2017937611.

CCSS: RI.1.1, 2, 4, 5, 6, 7; RI.2.2, 5, 6, 7, 10; RI.3.1, 5, 7, 8; RF.1.1, 3, 4; RF.2.3, 4

First Edition HC 9 8 7 6 5 4 3 2 1
First Edition PBK 9 8 7 6 5 4 3 2 1

Table of Contents

Concrete Mixer Beginnings 4

Revolving Drums 7

Concrete Plants 11

Mixing Variety 12

Wheeling Around 15

Concrete Mixers at Work 16

Amazing Concrete Mixers 20

Concrete Mixer Blueprint 22

Read More 24

Websites 24

Index 24

Before concrete mixer trucks were common, portable mixers worked with other machines to spread concrete.

For thousands of years, **concrete** has been used in construction. It used to be mixed by hand. In the early 1900s, concrete mixer trucks were made. Large drums held concrete. Over time, mixers got bigger.

concrete a mixture of aggregate (crushed stone, gravel, or sand), cement, and water

Today's concrete mixers can move more than 32,000 pounds (14,515 kg) of concrete. The steel drum is strong. It is always spinning. Inside, screw-shaped fins push wet concrete around. This keeps it from hardening.

Concrete usually takes about six days to completely cure, or harden.

The drum turns in the opposite direction to pour. Some drums tilt upward, too. Wet concrete runs down a chute. The chute is usually four or five feet (1.2–1.5 m) in length.

Chute extensions can be attached to drop concrete farther away from the truck.

About 75 percent of the concrete used today is ready-mix concrete made at plants.

Many drums are loaded with wet concrete at a **plant**. Then concrete mixers drive to a worksite. They pour the concrete within an hour of mixing it.

plant a place where manufacturing processes happen

Concrete boom trucks (right) pump concrete through a hose to the upper levels of buildings.

Volumetric mixers carry cement, **aggregate**, and water separately. They mix concrete at the building site. The fresh concrete is poured right away. Pumps can send wet concrete to upper stories of buildings.

aggregate crushed stone, gravel, or sand

Concrete mixers travel on roads. Many go from a concrete plant to a construction site. Others stay at the worksite. The truck's big wheels take the mixer wherever it is needed.

Concrete mixers are sometimes called transit mixers because they mix concrete as they move.

Rear-dispensing mixers need two operators. One stays in the cab. The other pushes the chute as it pours. Some mixers pour from a front chute. The driver uses a computer to control this chute.

A worker pushes the chute so that it does not drop too much concrete in one spot.

Rear-dispensing

trucks dump wet concrete at road worksites. Workers smooth it out before it dries.

Workers smooth large areas of concrete with a tool called a bull float.

Concrete mixers deliver concrete to worksites. The concrete is used to make roads and sidewalks. It helps build bridges, homes, dams, and playgrounds. Look for a concrete mixer the next time you see a worksite!

Concrete mixers work with other large machines like tower cranes.

Concrete Mixer Blueprint

hopper

mixing drum

chute

chute extension

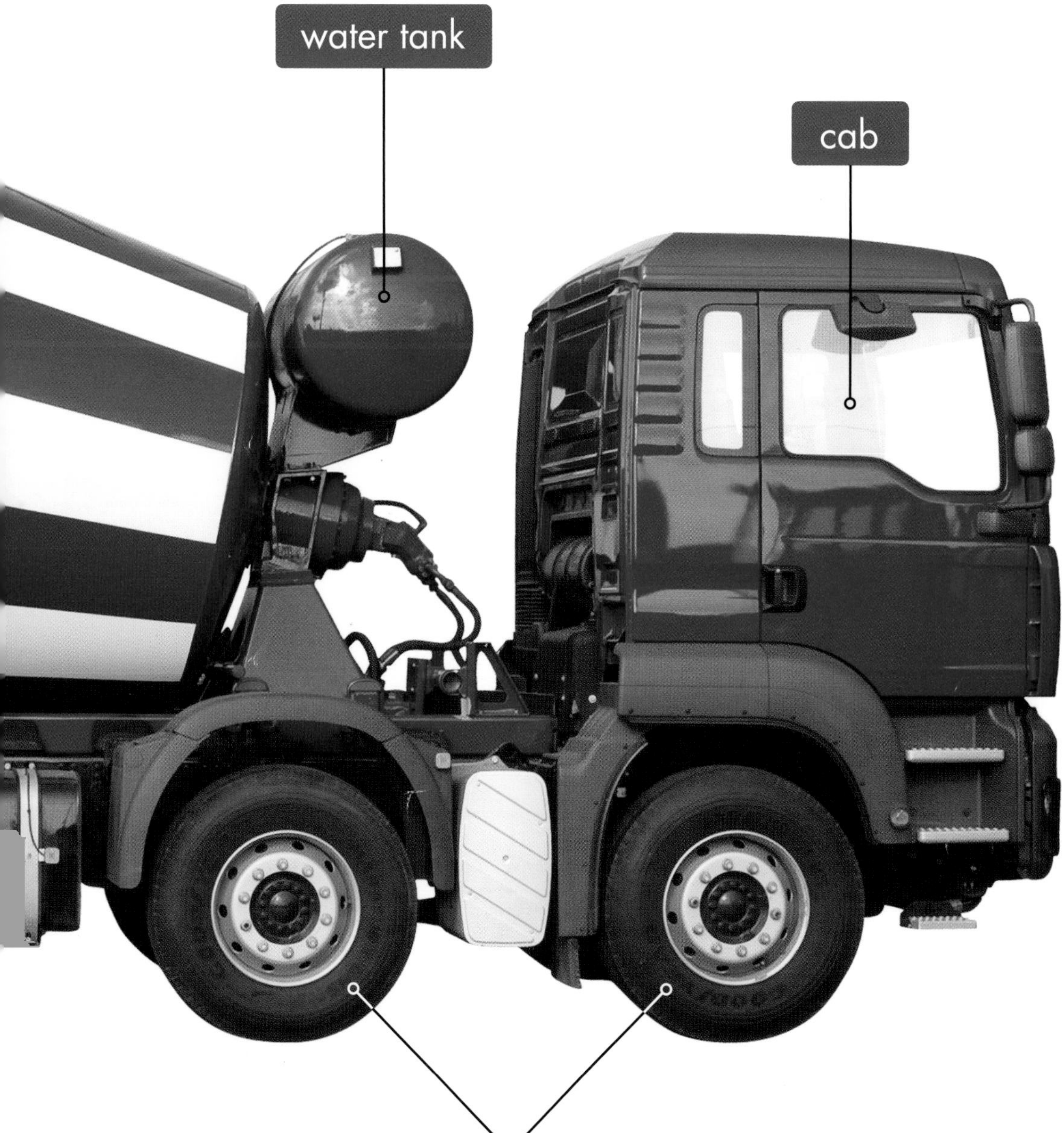

water tank

cab

wheels

Read More

Lennie, Charles. *Concrete Mixers*. Minneapolis: Abdo Kids, 2015.

Pettiford, Rebecca. *Concrete Mixers*. Minneapolis: Bellwether Media, 2018.

Schuh, Mari. *Concrete Mixers*. North Mankato, Minn.: Amicus, 2018.

Websites

Concrete Network: Timeline of Concrete and Cement History
https://www.concretenetwork.com/concrete-history/
Learn more about how concrete has been used throughout history.

Twin Cities PBS: Hoover Dam: Moving the Concrete
http://www.tpt.org/american-experience/episode/hoover-dam-moving-the-concrete/
See how construction crews moved millions of tons of concrete.

Note: Every effort has been made to ensure that the websites listed above are suitable for children, that they have educational value, and that they contain no inappropriate material. However, because of the nature of the Internet, it is impossible to guarantee that these sites will remain active indefinitely or that their contents will not be altered.

Index

aggregate 12
cement 12
chutes 8, 16
drums 4, 7, 8, 11
fins 7
operators 16
plants 11, 15
pouring 8, 11, 12, 16, 19
pumps 12
volumetric mixers 12
water 12
wheels 15